£6.20

Invaders
THE ROMANS

JILL HONNYWILL

Contents

	Page
Introduction	2
The Romans	3
The Invasions	4
Queen Boudica	7
Building Hadrian's Wall	11
The Chance to Change	12
Living in a Country Villa	12
Farming	14
Towns and Trade	16
Slaves	20
Schools	21
Roman Transport	22
A Roman fort	24
Gods and Goddesses	26
Daring to be a Christian	27
How long did the Romans stay?	28
Thinking back	30
After the Romans	31
The Anglo-Saxons	31
Christians	33
King Alfred	35
The Vikings Arrive!	36
Vikings All Around	39
Glossary	40
Index	IBC

Introduction

In this book we are going to go back a long way in time to find out what Britain was like then and who the early people were who came to live here. They are some of our **ancestors,** or relations from long ago. Some of them came peacefully but most of them were soldiers and raiders. They invaded and fought to gain some land. When they felt safe they settled down to farm and their families came to join them.

We have some ideas or **evidence** about what life was like then from things found by **archaeologists** in Britain and in other lands, from carvings on people's tombstones and from the few historians who were writing then.

The Romans

The Romans came from Italy. They invaded many lands and ruled over them. It was called the Roman **Empire**. The leader of the Romans was called the Emperor who lived in Rome. This map shows the Roman Empire just before the Romans first came to Britain.

The Invasions

Julius Caesar was a very important Roman general. He kept a record so that the people back in Rome would know how well he had done.

We know from his records that in 55 **BC** he attacked the Celts in Britain. Caesar wanted to attack Britain because the Celts there were helping the people of Gaul to fight against him. He also wanted the silver, gold and tin from the mines in Britain.

▲ Carving showing Roman soldiers using a 'fighting tortoise' tactic in a battle.

When Caesar's fleet of ships arrived the Celts were watching for them on the shore in their war chariots. The Romans landed but in a few weeks Caesar went back because the Celts kept attacking his men when they left their camp to look for food.

Julius Caesar did not give up. The next year he came back with a bigger army. No-one was waiting for him. This time he made friends with the enemies of the Celtic king. They told him where the king's stronghold was and showed him the secret paths into it. Caesar wrote that the stronghold was "protected by forests and marshes and the Celts had 4 000 chariots and lots of men."

Caesar won the battle and made peace. He took some hostages and demanded some taxes to be paid to Rome. Then he went away.

The third try

The third time the Romans came to Britain was is **AD** 43. The Roman Emperor Claudius sent his general, Plautius, to invade Britain. This time the Romans won and they stayed here.

Here are some reasons why the Romans were stronger this time.

A The Romans had strong allies. King Verica from Hampshire wanted to help them.
B The Roman Emperor Claudius ordered the invasion. Claudius was very keen to win to show the people in Rome how powerful he was.
C The Celtic people were not waiting to attack him when he arrived.
D The Roman army was very big. There were 24 000 soldiers and plenty of helpers.
E Claudius put his best general, Plautius, in charge.
F Plautius captured the Celtic capital, Colchester, easily.

Plautius made Colchester his safe headquarters and then his army set out to conquer the rich parts of Britain. The Romans wanted the good farmland and the mines to give them precious metals.

Most Celts lived in simple wooden houses but some of them were hidden in great forts like Maiden Castle. People would go into these in times of danger.

▲ What a Celtic hut would have looked like.

▶ Maiden castle – a huge hill fort.

The Romans used their **ballistas** which fired metal bolts over the earth banks and killed the Celts. This was a new kind of technology in Britain.

The Romans stopped conquering when they got to the Fosse Way. They built forts but were often attacked from Wales. The Romans decided to take Wales and kill the **Druids** who had gone to live on the Isle of Anglesey. They were clever priests who would not obey the Romans. Their followers had to do as they said and not to listen to the Romans. This made the Romans angry.

It was then, in AD 60, that there was a large **revolt** against the Romans by one of the Celtic tribes.

ACTIVITIES

1 Caesar wrote his diary so that people in Rome would think that he was brave and clever. Do you think that he always wrote the truth? Do you think that the Celts had 4 000 chariots?

2 Look at the picture of the Roman soldiers on page 4. Why do you think this is called a fighting tortoise? Why did the Romans fight like this?

3 In small groups put the reasons for the Roman success in AD 43 on page 5 in order of importance. Do all the groups agree?

4 Why do you think that the Romans wanted the rich farmland and the mines?

5 Why were the Druids a danger to the Romans?

6 The Romans first came to Britain in 55 BC. They came to stay in AD 43. How many years later was this? Your glossary will help you.

Queen Boudica

This is a story of the revolt in AD 60 against the Roman invaders by the Iceni tribe who lived not far from Colchester. At the end of the story you can find out how we know about it. The places in the story are marked on the map to help you follow it.

7

ONE DAY THE OLD KING of the Iceni made a plan. He said that when he died his wife, Boudica, would rule and the Romans would help her. Soon after he died and the Queen and her two girls were very sad.

Some Roman soldiers came from Colchester. They wanted the kingdom for the Roman Emperor. The Queen and her chiefs tried to explain that the land belonged to them. But the Romans took all the land and treasures.

Boudica called for an army and many Celts came. The Romans had taken their land and made them pay taxes. Boudica marched to attack Roman Colchester. She ambushed Romans marching to help Colchester. Her women went into the town and spread rumours which frightened the people. Her army made a circle round the town. They attacked and killed people and burnt Colchester down. Then they marched on to London.

The Londoners sent messengers to ask the Roman General Paulinus to help them. His army was just about to attack the Druids in Anglesey. Paulinus and a few soldiers galloped very quickly to London. Paulinus reached London before Boudica but his army could not get there in time. He told the people that he could not help. Then he went back up Watling Street.

Many people ran away from London. Soon Boudica arrived and captured the city. Her army killed a lot of people and set London on fire. Then Boudica's army marched up Watling Street to Verulamium and did the same thing. There were no Romans in Verulamium but they killed all the Celts because they had been friendly with the Romans.

More people joined Boudica's army. They wanted to drive the Romans out of Britain. They went up Watling street to find Paulinus.

Paulinus had been busy. He stopped where Watling Street crossed the Fosse Way. He sent messages for more soldiers to come. There was not much time.

▲ A model of a Roman soldier.

Paulinus picked a good spot for the battle. His men blocked the road at the end of a narrow valley with steep hills with woods around them. In front the road went along the valley and then into a large field. The Romans could hear Boudica's army coming.

Boudica's army did not march smartly with each group following its leader like the Romans. They came as a great mass of men bringing their families to watch. They had a much bigger army than the Romans. They made plenty of noise. They were sure they would win. They put the family wagons round the sides of the field near the trees.

Boudica's army of war chariots and foot soldiers rushed at the small Roman army. There was not room for them all in the narrow valley. The Romans threw their javelins and hit the front men. Boudica's men got into a panic and fell over each other.

The Romans took their swords and slowly moved forward. Boudica's men wanted to run away but the family carts were in the way. The Roman horsemen chased after them. The chariots got stuck in the woods. The Romans killed everyone they saw. They did not find Boudica but they never heard of her again. They were told she did not want to be captured so she poisoned herself.

Boudica and the Celts did not write the story. A Roman officer called Agricola was in Britain at the time. Years later he told his son-in-law, Tacitus who wrote it down.

ACTIVITIES

1 Tacitus was a Roman. Do you think he wrote a fair story?

2 Copy the map on page 7 or see the Teacher's Guide. Can you mark in Boudica's marches in one colour and Paulinus' in another?

3 Make a list of why the Romans won or why Boudica's army lost.

4 Can you think how you could check up on the burning of London? What would we look for?

5 Can you act out this story?

Building Hadrian's Wall

After Queen Boudica's rebellion the Romans had no more trouble. Twenty years later they had made everyone in Britain obey them. They built forts at Chester and near Newport to keep control. Tacitus went on with his story about Agricola who became the governor of Britain. Tacitus wrote that Agricola even invaded Scotland with his army but it was too far to take food and there were many ambushes.

When the Emperor Hadrian came to Britain in AD 122 he told the army to build a wall from Tynemouth to Carlisle to defend Britain. It took about four years to build and later they made it even stronger.

▼ Hadrian's wall.

The chance to change

The Celts had to choose. Some went to live away from the Romans, on the high ground in the western parts of Britain. But many of them stayed to learn Roman ways and to become rich. They spoke Latin, wore the same sorts of clothes and worshipped the same gods. Soon it was hard to know if they were Romans or Celts.

Living in a Country Villa

Villas were large Roman houses. We know about these houses from archaeology. Here is a villa in Pompeii, near Rome. The house was built around a garden and had four sides. The family lived in one side, the slaves in another and the rest was for stores and offices. The garden had trees for shade, herbs for cooking, flowers and sometimes a fountain. There were houses like this in Britain.

The house of Vetti.

Inside the villa the Romans liked bright colours and lots of pictures which they painted on the walls. Sometimes these were of trees and animals or they told stories about the Roman gods and goddesses.

We know about the furniture they had from these paintings and carvings, and also from archaeology. A stool like the one in the picture was dug up in Italy.

▶ The Museum of London have made this Roman dining room.

On the floor they had mosaics made of lots of tiny pieces of coloured glass or stone which make patterns. Some of the best mosaics have been found at Fishbourne, which was a great palace in the south of England.

▲ A floor mosaic at the palace at Fishbourne.

ACTIVITIES

1 Look at the Roman furniture. What is different about our rooms to-day?

2 Can you design and make your own mosaic. There are others in this book to look at before you begin.

3 Look back to page 5 and find the picture of the Celtic hut. Is it like the Roman villa? What is different about it?

Farming

▲ A carving showing men ploughing with a couple of oxen.

The Romans often set up very big farms around the country villas. They grew corn and sold it to the Roman army. Some corn was sent away to other parts of the Roman Empire in boats. They also sold meat, fruit and animal skins called hides. They kept sheep and used the wool. Some farms had a place to make and repair iron tools.

Sometimes farms were so big that fifty families worked there. The Celtic farmers who had lived there before the invasion now paid rent to the Romans. They worked on the farms.

▼ A model of the palace at Fishbourne.

Eating

▲ A place setting at a Roman table.

Women had a lot of jobs in the villa-farms – most of them were indoors. The lady often had the help of slaves. She planned the food and told the cook what to do. Rich Romans liked to have visitors. They had great feasts but they did not sit on chairs to eat. They lay on sofas in a circle with the food in the middle.

Roman cookery books which have been found tell us the kinds of food Romans ate. They often started with shellfish like oysters, or eggs. Then they had meat with a very strong fish gravy over it and leeks and onions – but no potatoes. They drank wine and had fruit at the end of dinner.

ACTIVITIES

1 How do you think we know about the Roman villa-farms?

2 Here is a list of things that need to be done to wool before it can be made into clothes. Can you put them in the right order?

dying   sheering   weaving   washing   spinning

3 Make up and design a menu for a Roman feast.

4 Why did they not have potatoes? Look at the picture of the place setting – what is missing?

5 Here is a Roman recipe for dates which you could try and make.

Stone the dates and stuff them with nuts (almonds and walnuts are best). Sprinkle salt over the dates. Fry gently in honey for three or four minutes and serve hot or cold.

15

Towns and trade

The Celts had lived in small villages. Towns were a new idea in Britain. The Roman writer Tacitus tells us that ten new towns were built by Agricola, the Roman Governor from AD 75 to AD 90.

▲ A street in the Roman town of Pompeii in Italy.

We know a little about how the towns looked and what they had because archaeologists have dug them up in Britain. Roman towns in Britain were very like Roman towns in Gaul or Italy and so we can learn from the archaeologists there too.

The towns had paved streets, water ran in pipes and they had good drains. There was a big market place called the forum where fruit and vegetables from the villa-farms were sold. There were workshops nearby where the craftsmen made many useful and beautiful things to sell.

Traders travelled from one market to the next. They sold tools, pottery and wine from Gaul as well as food and things from Britain.

The towns had big buildings like a town hall. People went there to pay taxes and law breakers were tried there.

▲ A carving showing a shop selling knives.

▶ A carving showing a fruit and vegetable shop.

▼ A Roman butcher's shop.

17

Going out

The Romans built large public baths in the towns. People went there to meet their friends and also because they wanted to be clean.

At Bath, the Romans found a hot spring and built several baths there including this swimming pool. They used stone pillars to make it look beautiful and to hold up the high roof which was made of wood and tiles.

▲ The Roman baths at Bath.

If there was no hot spring the Romans used an underground heating system to heat the water and the rooms. There was a hot room which was very steamy, a warm room and a cold room.

There was sometimes an **amphitheatre** in the towns where Romans could watch wrestling, men fighting wild animals and chariot races.

▲ The amphitheatre of Emperor Flavius in Italy.

Clothes

The Romans liked to look smart when they went out. Hair styles changed but it was always important to have it tied back to show the beautiful outline of the face.

The Roman writer, Tacitus, writes that the toga was seen everywhere in Britain. The toga was a large piece of cloth worn over a tunic. It went over one shoulder and under the other arm.

▲ This tombstone shows a man wearing a toga.

ACTIVITIES

1 Look at all the pictures in this chapter. What is different about towns today? What is the same? Think about shopping and going out.

2 What are taxes? Can you find out?

3 Are the Roman baths like your local swimming baths? What is different and what is the same?

4 How did the Romans dress? Look at all the pictures in this book first. You can write or draw your answer.

Slaves

Rich Romans could buy people and own them. They were called slaves. There were slaves in Britain before the Romans came.

Sometimes the Romans were cruel to them and made them work very, very hard and did not pay them. Some worked in the mines and some rowed the **galleys**.

▶ A mosaic showing a slave in a Roman kitchen.

Some slaves were lucky and worked for kind Roman families. They could buy and sell things and when they had lots of money they could pay their master and be free. If a master married a slave girl she was free. Sometimes a kind master would make a slave free.

ACTIVITIES

1 The Celts and the Romans were happy to have slaves. Do you think slavery is wrong? Why?

2 What do you think the people had done to become slaves?

Schools

Girls and boys went to school at seven years old. It was not free so some children did not go. The schools were mainly in the towns. In the country, rich children had lessons at home with a teacher. Books for the children were made by tying small flat bits of wood together like a concertina. Wax was poured on and then set. Children wrote on the wax with a bronze stylus and used the blunt end to rub out.

▶ A wax writing tablet and stili.

Latin

The Roman language was called Latin. Children learnt to read and write in Latin at school. When the Romans went away from Britain they left a lot of people who had learned to read and write Latin.

We still have words which come from Latin words. The words are often to do with armies, roads and the Romans' favourite foods. Some towns still have the names the Romans gave them.

ACTIVITIES

1 Here is a list of Latin words. Copy them into your book. Put one word on each line near the margin. Beside each word write what you guess it means. Check with your friends and then ask your teacher.

schola   exit   tabula   vestis   milia   cupa   circus
triangulum   cubus   strata   vinum

21

Roman transport

The Romans did not feel very safe. The Picts and Scots often attacked Britain (see pages 28-29). The Romans wanted riders to tell them about attacks quickly. Then the soldiers marched to fight them.

To do this the Romans needed good roads and they took care where they made them. They stood on a hill top and looked for the shortest way to reach the next hill. Often the roads went in lines like a ruler. To cross rivers they looked for a narrow bit of a river to make a short bridge.

▲ A Roman road in Yorkshire.

We know how the roads were made because a Roman wrote about what they did.

> The first thing is to dig a deep trench in the ground. The second is to refill the trench with other materials to make a strong base for the road. . . . The ground must not give way . . . when people and carts go over it. Paving stones are put on top and held in with wedges.

We still use some of the Roman roads today.

The new towns and the soldiers in Britain all needed a lot of supplies. At first, most of these supplies had to be imported from other parts of the Roman Empire and came to ports in Britain by boat. Then they were put in barges and taken up the rivers. This Roman barge was found in the mud at London.

▼ The remains of a Roman barge

▲ A wall painting showing a Roman boat.

ACTIVITIES

1 What supplies do you think came to Britain? Can you remember some of the things that came to the town markets from Gaul? Look back to check.

2 Why do you think the Romans used water transport?

3 What can you learn from the two different pieces of evidence on this page about barges? Which do you think is the more important piece of evidence? Look at the pictures carefully and draw a Roman barge.

A Roman fort

The Romans made forts to defend the parts of Britain which they had invaded. One was called Vindolanda.

Archaeologists dug up the rubbish tip at the fort and found all kinds of things. Over 800 Roman writing tablets were found. These were thin pieces of wood tied together. When the archaeologists put the wood under a special lamp they saw writing in ink on them. There were letters, army documents and records.

We can learn that the soldiers living in the fort wrote to families and friends. Vindolanda was a long way from the large towns. The soldiers often asked people to send them things they would need. Here is part of a letter to a soldier.

> I have sent you socks from Sattua, two pairs of sandals and two sets of underpants.

The Romans had men called scribes who wrote letters for them. This letter was written by a scribe. It is a birthday invitation from Claudia to her friend Sulpicia.

▼ A piece from a writing tablet made from wood.

Look down in the bottom right-hand corner. That is the bit written by Claudia herself and it is the earliest bit of writing by a Roman woman ever found. It was written about AD 100.

> I send you an invitation to come to us on September 11th for my birthday party which will be more fun if you came. Give my love to your husband. My husband sends his love to you and your sons.

ACTIVITIES

1 Imagine you are far away from home. Write a letter to your family asking for things to be sent to you. What would you ask for? Design and make a folding letter like the wooden tablets found at Vindolanda.

2 What does finding a birthday party invitation tell you about life in a Roman fort?

3 Imagine that Sulpicia goes to visit Claudia for the party. Can you write a story about the dangerous adventures Sulpicia might have had on her journey to the party?

4 You know a lot about the things the Romans used. Make a list of other things that might have been found at Vindolanda.

Gods and Goddesses

The Romans had a lot of different gods and goddesses. Some had been invented by the Greeks. The Romans called the king of the gods, Jupiter and the queen, Juno.

The Romans often put an altar to a god or goddess in the town hall. When they wanted to ask the gods or thank them for something they took gifts to the gods. Sometimes they killed an animal.

Both the Romans and the Celts were often buried with their own favourite treasures beside them in their graves. These things were found in a child's grave at Colchester.

▶ A drawing of Roman vessels and figures found in a grave.

The Celtic people also had a lot of gods. The Romans were happy to join them together. The Roman war god was called Mars. The Celtic war gods were called Lenus and Alator and so in Roman Britain they became Mars Lenus and Mars Alator.

The Romans did not like Celtic gods and goddesses that did not match theirs. The Celts had a goddess called Andrasta which meant unbeatable. Her priests were the Druids who did not like the Romans.

Daring to be a Christian

Jesus died in Palestine, part of the Roman Empire, in about AD 33. It took time for his followers, the Christians, to reach Rome. They were not popular there as they did not worship Roman Gods and the Emperor said they must be killed.

Romans still became Christians but had to keep it secret. Some of them came to Britain in the army. By AD 200, some Celts began worshipping Jesus and became secret Christians. Secret marks made by Christians have been found on pots, plates and cups in Britain. They made up a code using the first two letters of Christ in the Greek language.

▶ A Roman mosaic found in a villa in Dorset showing Christ. It is the only Roman picture of Christ that has been found in Britain.

In AD 313 in Rome there was a great change. The Emperor Constantine became a Christian and said that Christianity was to be the main religion of the Romans.

ACTIVITIES

1 Can you find out about some more Roman gods? Why do you think the Romans and Greeks invented gods and goddesses and worshipped them?

2 Do you think the Christians were pleased in AD 313? What difference do you think it made to their lives?

How long did the Romans stay?

The Romans had made Britain safe. They had made Hadrian's Wall to keep out invaders. They had a lot of soldiers. Britain was rich and sent wool and corn and silver to Rome in ships.

However, there were pirates at sea. They attacked the ships. The Romans had to have a fleet to fight the pirates and build forts like Porchester. They built a lighthouse at Dover to help their ships. It all cost a lot of money.

▶ The lighthouse at Dover.

Then, in AD 351, the Emperor started taking away the soldiers from Britain to fight in other parts of the Empire. The Picts found out and made more attacks. Then they had a new idea. In AD 367, instead of attacking Hadrian's Wall, they got into boats and went round each end and then landed. They were then behind the soldiers on the wall. Attacks also came from all sides across the sea.

The people in Britain wanted to help the Romans. They could not because only the army had weapons. The attackers were beaten back this time but more and more soldiers were leaving Britain. In the end, in AD 412, the people of Britain sent a letter to the Emperor. They asked for help. The Emperor Honorious sent a letter back. He said they must look after themselves. Soon pottery factories closed and buildings built by the Romans began to fall apart. Archaeologists have found out that no more new coins came from Rome or Gaul.

The Romans had gone and they did not come back.

ACTIVITIES

1 How do you think the archaeologists know about the forts the Romans built?

2 Why do you think the people in Britain were not allowed to carry weapons?

3 Can you make a story like a comic strip to tell the story of the Romans going?

4 Do you think the Romans left because of the mistakes they made or because of things other people did? Make two lists and then decide.

5 What do you think happened after the Romans stopped defending Britain from attack and went away?

Thinking Back

In this book there are lots of different kinds of evidence. They are proofs that the Romans were here and that they did many things.

ACTIVITIES

1 Invite some visitors into your classroom. You must prove to them that the Romans did come to Britain. Make a list of all the things you can tell them. Decide which pieces of evidence were the most helpful. Put them in order – the most important first.

2 What piece of evidence would you most like to find which tells you something new about the Romans in Britain?

After the Romans

After the Romans left there were lots of different leaders. They all ruled a bit of Britain. There was no big army to stop the Picts and Scots and Anglo-Saxon pirates from attacking. It was all very worrying.

A man called Vortigern became leader. 'Vortigern' means leader. He still did not have a big army. It was now about forty years after the Romans had left Britain. Vortigern promised to pay soldiers from Europe to chase the Picts and Scots out. The soldiers he asked to help were the Angles and Saxons.

The Anglo-Saxons

Vortigern had no money. He had to give the Anglo-Saxons land and food as payment. The Anglo-Saxons told their friends and relations and soon they came to Britain too. They did not want to go home.

The Celts thought there were too many Anglo-Saxons and there were battles between them. Some Celts went back to live in the hills. They had their own leader. Perhaps he was King Arthur.

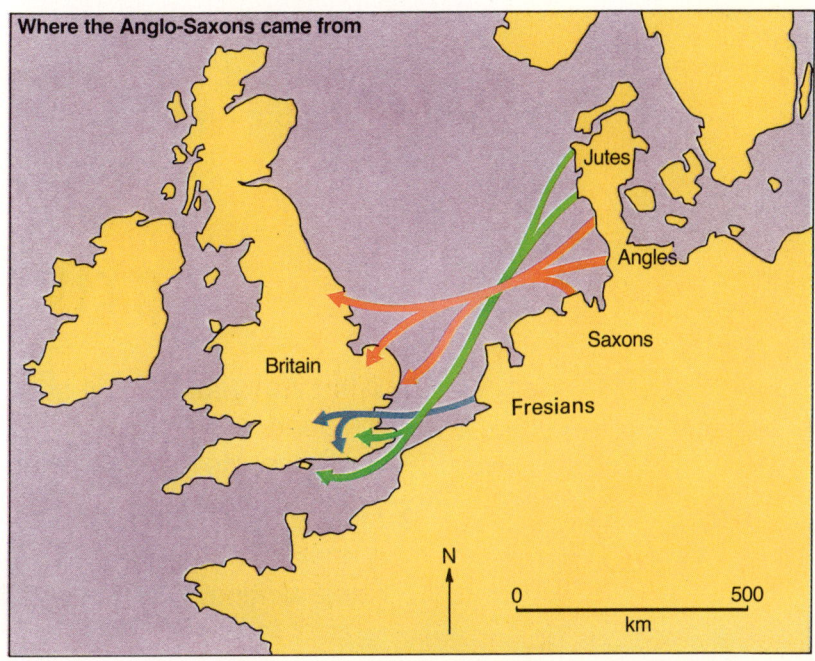

Where the Anglo-Saxons came from

▲ A reconstructed Anglo-Saxon house.

▶ A reconstructed village scene.

The Anglo-Saxons and the Celts had battles, but by AD 550 the Anglo-Saxons had won. They were in Britain to stay.

The Anglo-Saxons wanted to be farmers so they stayed on the low land. They did not want to live in the big villas. They liked their warm wooden houses that did not need so many servants.

Soon they lived peacefully beside the Celts. Sometimes they took farms from the Celts. Sometimes they lived in farms left by the Romans or empty farms where families had died of plague. They did not live in towns and buy things. So the craftsmen and shopkeepers in the towns had to go and grow food for their families in the country.

Britain changed. More people lived in the country on farms. The big towns were left empty.

ACTIVITIES

1 What can you find out about King Arthur? Is he just a legend or was he real? Ask your teacher for the evidence. How will you decide?

2 Look at all the different houses in this book. Make a chart to compare them. Draw pictures and do some writing. Can you find out more about them?

Christians

Do you remember that some of the Roman soldiers had been Christians? After they left some people went on being Christian. These Christians were looked after by **monks** from Wales, Scotland and Ireland. These monks were poor, holy men. They could read and write when most other people could not. One of the most famous was St Patrick of Ireland. Some Anglo-Saxon leaders became Christian too.

Many Anglo-Saxons were **pagans**. They had their own family of gods. There was Woden, king of the gods; Tiw, the god of war and Thor, the god of thunder and the sky. Back in Rome the Pope said he was the head of all the Christians. Pope Gregory sent one of his monks, called Augustine, to turn the Anglo-Saxons into Christians.

▲ Pope Gregory.

▶ Part of a bronze helmet showing an Anglo-Saxon god.

Augustine was proud and grand. He came to England in his best robes, with his followers singing behind him. At the same time the poorer Celtic Christians came to Britain to tell people to become Christian.

The two groups did not get on with each other. In the end the King of Northumbria chose the Roman Christians in AD 664. After this the Roman church rules began to be used all over Britain.

Britain gradually became a Christian country, following the Pope in Rome.

ACTIVITIES

1 Can you find out more about St Patrick?

2 Why do you think the Celtic Christians did not like St Augustine?

3 What different religions are there in Britain today?

King Alfred

Alfred's father was king of Wessex. Most boys did not learn lessons but Alfred learnt to read and write. He went all the way to Rome to visit the Pope. When he became King he wanted his people to be good Christians and to be safe from invaders.

Alfred sorted out the old laws and made some new ones. He found men to be priests and wrote a book to teach bishops how to do their job.

Alfred wanted **chronicles** to be written so that people could read about what happened. He collected the old chronicles written by the monks in Latin. He asked his friend, Asser and some monks to translate the Chronicles into their English. They made copies of it. The copies were sent to different monasteries and the monks added to them each year, like a diary. They were called the Anglo-Saxon Chronicles.

▲ A statue of Alfred made long after he died.

ACTIVITIES

1 Make a list of why people need rules or laws. Why do they need to be changed?

2 Does your school keep a Chronicle. Is it true?

35

The Vikings Arrive!

The pagan Vikings were terrifying. They came across the North Sea in a new kind of fast boat. They attacked, robbed, set houses on fire and went away until next time.

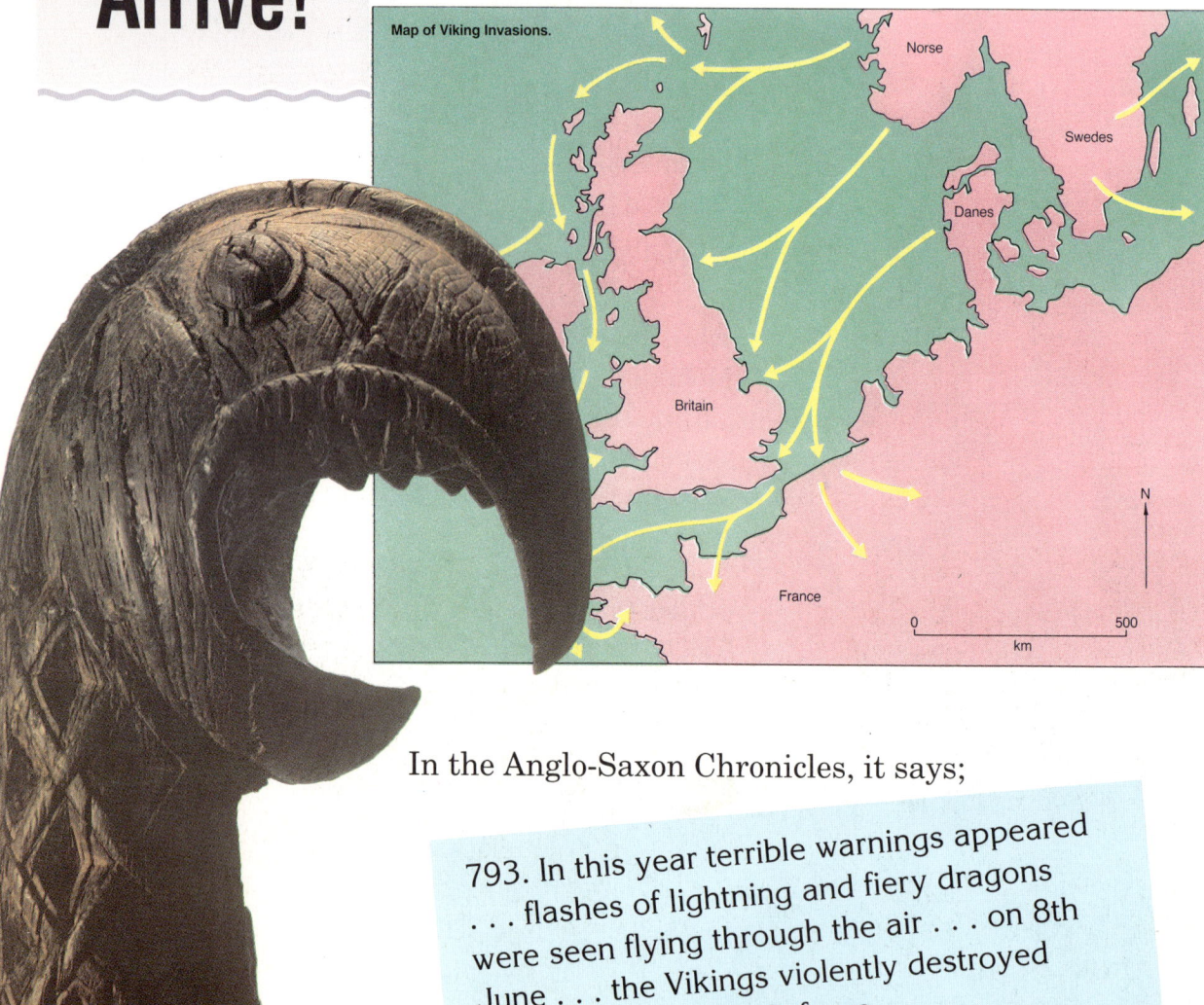

Map of Viking Invasions.

▲ Carving from a ship.

In the Anglo-Saxon Chronicles, it says;

> 793. In this year terrible warnings appeared . . . flashes of lightning and fiery dragons were seen flying through the air . . . on 8th June . . . the Vikings violently destroyed God's church of Lindisfarne.

The Vikings attacked in the summer. After sixty years they began to stay for the winter instead of going home. They began to kill Anglo-Saxon kings, like King Edmund of the East Angles. They took land and began to farm. They wanted more land and power and they took over other kingdoms, like Northumbria. The Vikings demanded money and treasure from the people. They called it **Danegeld**.

The Vikings wanted Wessex. King Alfred had made his army strong and he led the other kings in the battle against the Vikings. At Christmas in AD 877, the Viking leader Guthrum made a surprise attack and Alfred had to run away. But in the summer of AD 878 Alfred called up a big army. They beat Guthrum and made peace. Guthrum became a Christian. England was divided into two. The Vikings were allowed to keep Northumbria, East Anglia and part of Mercia. This was called **Danelaw.**

Alfred did not quite trust Guthrum so he made strong walls round his towns. If the Vikings attacked the people could go to the towns to be safe. The towns began to grow again.

The Vikings began to settle down and life became more peaceful. Most of them were farmers but they also lived in towns such as Jorvik. Here there were craftsmen, shopkeepers and traders.

▼ A street scene in Viking York which has been reconstructed at the Jorvik Museum.

ACTIVITIES

1 Read the story of the Viking attack from the Chronicles and make a collage or write a poem about it.

2 Write about the attack as if you were a Viking. Will it be the same?

3 How long after the Romans left did the Vikings attack?

Vikings All Around

The Vikings lived in Sweden, Norway and Denmark. They got in their fast boats and went to look for land and riches.

▶ A reconstruction of a Viking ship.

It was not just England that was raided and robbed. They went to many countries. In Russia they carried their boats over the land until they came to a big river which led them, in the end, to the great city of Constantinople. They carved their writing on stones which have been found. There is even a Viking **saga**, or story, which says they went to North America.

ACTIVITIES

1 Is a saga enough evidence to be sure that the Vikings went to North America?

2 Think about the Romans, the Anglo-Saxons and the Vikings. Why did they all become travellers and invaders. Was it for the same reason?

3 This book has been about one thousand years and lots of people. Would you have chosen to live with the Romans, the Anglo-Saxons or the Vikings? Why? Do you all agree? Work out how to tell the class why you chose your Invaders.

Glossary

AD — Years after the birth of Christ have AD next to them. See BC.

amphitheatre — Roman open air theatre where people went to see fighting and chariot races.

ancestor — A relative from long ago.

archaeologist — Someone who learns about the past, usually by digging things up.

BC — Before Christ. Years are counted from the birth of Christ. Years before this are counted backwards and have BC after them.

ballistas — Machines designed a long time ago to break down castle walls. They worked like giant catapults and fired small stones.

chronicle — List of what happened each year.

Druids — A religious group who were very powerful in Britain.

empire — A group of countries ruled by one person or government.

evidence — Something left from the past – includes writing, buildings, art, objects. If we look at them carefully they can give us proof about the past.

galleys — An old type of ship which was moved by sails and by people rowing with oars.

monks — Men who live in a religious group in a monastery.

pagan — Someone who believes in lots of gods and not in one of the main religions.

Picts — The tribe of people who lived in Scotland at the time of the Romans.

revolt — An uprising by the people against their rulers.

saga — A long story about a hero's adventures.